Mega Military Machines™
Megamáquinas militares™

CARS AND TRUCKS

AUTOS Y CAMIONES

Catherine Ellis

Traducción al español: María Cristina Brusca

PowerKiDS press. & **Editorial Buenas Letras**™

New York

Published in 2007 by The Rosen Publishing Group, Inc.
29 East 21st Street, New York, NY 10010

First Edition

Editor: Amelie von Zumbusch
Book Design: Greg Tucker
Layout Design: Lissette González

Photo Credits: Cover, pp. 5, 11 © Craig DeBourbon/iStockphoto.com; pp. 7, 9 Shutterstock.com; p. 13 by Tech. Sgt. H.H. Deffner; p. 15 by SSGT Shane A. Cuomo, U.S. Air Force; p. 17 © Hulton Archive/Getty Images; p. 19 by Don Sullivan; p. 21 by SPC Jory C. Randall; p. 23 by PFC Elizabeth Erste.

Cataloging Data

Ellis, Catherine
    Cars and trucks / Catherine Ellis; traducción al español: María Cristina Brusca. — 1st ed.
        p. cm. — (Mega military machines–Megamáquinas militares)
    Includes index.
    ISBN-13: 978-1-4042-7624-6 (library binding)
    ISBN-10: 1-4042-7624-6 (library binding)
    1. Vehicles, Military—Juvenile literature. 2. Armored vehicles, Military—Juvenile literature. 3. Spanish language materials. 4. Military trucks—Juvenile literature. I. Title.

Manufactured in the United States of America

Contents

Contenido

People in the military use special cars. They are bigger and stronger than everyday cars.

En el ejercito se usan autos especiales. Estos autos son más grandes y fuertes que los autos comunes.

The military also uses special trucks. The trucks often carry people, food, or **weapons**.

El ejército también usa camiones especiales. A menudo, los camiones llevan gente, comida o **armas**.

Military cars and trucks have big wheels. Their wheels let them be driven on or off the road.

Los autos y camiones militares tienen ruedas grandes. Estas ruedas les permiten andar dentro y fuera de los caminos.

9

Military cars and trucks have **armor**. This keeps the people inside them safe.

Los autos y camiones militares tienen **blindaje.** El blindaje protege a quienes viajan adentro.

Some military cars have big guns.

Algunos autos militares tienen armas grandes.

Soldiers drive military cars. This soldier is using **binoculars** to look around.

Los soldados conducen los autos militares. Este soldado está usando **binoculares** para mirar los alrededores.

This is a Ferret Scout Car. It is a small, fast military car.

Este es un Ferret Scout Car. Es un auto militar muy rápido y pequeño.

Soldiers can drive this military car into the water!

¡Los soldados pueden conducir este auto por el agua!

This is an Armored Personnel Carrier. It carries soldiers wherever they need to go.

Este es un transporte de soldados blindado. Se utiliza para llevar a los soldados de un lado a otro.

21

These military cars search places to make sure they are safe.

Estos autos militares revisan lugares para asegurarse de que no hay peligro.

23

Words to Know / Palabras que debes sabe

armor (AR-mer) A hard cover put over something to keep it safe.

binoculars (bih-NAH-kyuh-lurz) Handheld lenses that make things seem closer.

weapons (WEH-punz) Objects used to hurt or kill.

---

armas (las) Objetos que se usan para herir o matar.

binoculares (los) Lentes especiales que hacen que las cosas se vean más cerca.

blindaje (el) Cubierta dura que se pone sobre algo para protegerlo.

Index

A
armor, 10

B
binoculars, 14

S
soldier(s), 14, 18, 20

W
weapons, 6

Índice

A
armas, 6

B
binoculares, 14
blindaje, 10

S
soldado(s), 14, 18, 20